ABRAHAM LINCOLN

A Man for All the People

A Ballad by Myra Cohn Livingston

Illustrated by Samuel Byrd

Holiday House/New York

A man for all the people,
A man who stood up tall,
Abe Lincoln spoke of justice
And liberty for all.

Born in a log cabin
Work was what he knew,
Helped chop trees, plant corn, split logs.
Abe just grew and grew.

Abe moved to Indiana,
Abe moved to Illinois.
Always spent time reading
Since he was a boy.

Settled in New Salem
When he was twenty-one,
Worked awhile at clerking.
Abe's manhood had begun.

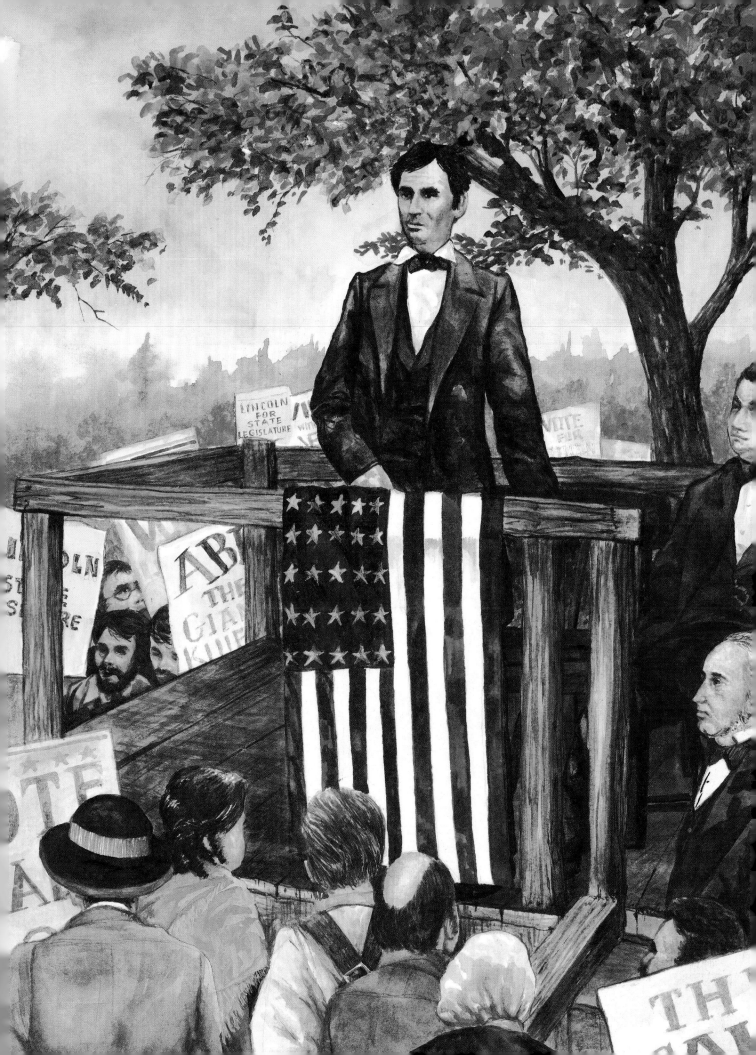

Tried to run for office,
Learned how to survey,
Wrestled and debated,
Kept learning every day.

Abe Lincoln was a lawyer,
Respected all the laws.
Rode the circuit fighting
For every human cause.

Moved again to Springfield.
People liked his looks.
Married Mary, had four sons,
Kept on reading books.

Abe went into politics,
Called slavery a blight,
Debated Stephen Douglas
With faith that "Right makes Might."

Abe was fun and witty,
Abe was moody, sad;
Spoke up for the good things,
Spoke against the bad.

Abe Lincoln ran for president.
He heard his country's call
Believing that "the people's will"
Should be the law for all.

Abe moved into the White House.
He sought equality.
He said, "All persons held as slaves
Henceforward shall be free."

Abe Lincoln was our president
All through the Civil War.
He knew the "fiery trial" ahead,
What men were fighting for.

Abe Lincoln spoke at Gettysburg.
He wrote a nation free
"Shall not perish from the earth."
Abe loved democracy.

"Fondly do we hope," he said,
"Fervently do we pray
That this mighty scourge of war
May speedily pass away."

Abe Lincoln led his generals,
And prayed the war would cease.
"Bind up the nation's wounds," he said,
"Cherish a lasting peace."

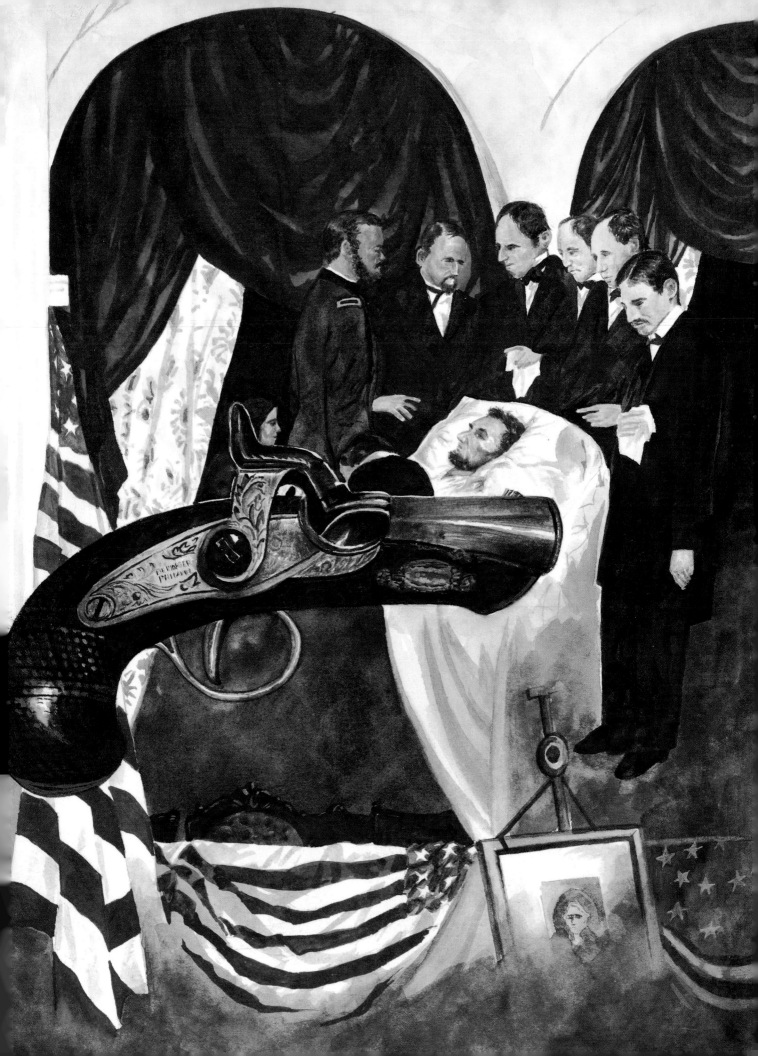

Abe knew he was in danger.
He dreamed that he was dead.
He went to see a play one night.
Booth shot him in the head.

IN THIS TEMPLE
AS IN THE HEARTS OF THE PEOPLE
FOR WHOM HE SAVED THE UNION
HE MEMORY OF ABRAHAM LINCOLN
IS ENSHRINED FOREVER

Abe Lincoln was a strong man
True to the people's will.
Tall, like his marble statue,
He sits among us still.

A man for all the people,
A man who stood up tall.
Abe Lincoln honored justice
And liberty for all.

The artwork on the pages listed below depicts the following scenes:

page 4: Chopping wood in front of the log cabin where he was born near Hodgeville, Kentucky, on February 12, 1809.

page 8: Working as a store clerk after moving to New Salem, Illinois in 1831.

page 24: Delivering the Gettysburg Address on November 19, 1863.

page 26: Meeting with General George B. McClellan on October 1, 1862.

page 28: After being shot by John Wilkes Booth at a performance at Ford's Theater on April 14, 1865.

page 30: Lincoln's statue in the Lincoln Memorial in Washington, D.C., sculpted by Daniel Chester French and dedicated in May, 1922.

The quoted passages in the text come from the following sources:

page 17: "Right makes Might" from an address at Cooper Institute, New York City, February 27, 1860.

page 19: "the people's will" from impromptu remarks, October 19, 1864.

page 21: "All persons held as slaves/ Henceforward shall be free" from the Emancipation Proclamation, January 1, 1863.

page 23: "fiery trial" from the State of the Union message to Congress, December 1, 1862.

page 25: "Shall not perish from the earth" from the Gettysburg Address, November 19, 1863.

page 27: "Fondly do we hope/Fervently do we pray/That this mighty scourge of war/May speedily pass away./Bind up the nation's wounds/Cherish a lasting peace" from the second Inaugural Address, March 4, 1865.

To John Briggs, Margery Cuyler,
and all the wonderful staff at Holiday House
for believing in me. Thank you.

S. B.

Library of Congress Cataloging-in-Publication Data
Livingston, Myra Cohn.
Abraham Lincoln : a man for all the people : a ballad / by Myra Cohn Livingston ;
illustrated by Samuel Byrd. — 1st ed.
p.   cm.
Summary: A narrative poem chronicling the life of the Civil War president.
ISBN 0-8234-1049-8
1. Lincoln, Abraham, 1809–1865 — Juvenile poetry. 2. Children's poetry,
American. [1. Lincoln. Abraham, 1809–1865 — Poetry. 2. Presidents — Poetry.
3. Narrative poetry. 4. American poetry.] I. Byrd, Samuel, ill. II. Title.
PS3562.I945A64   1993   93-2731   CIP   AC
811'.54 — dc20